M000302732

INTRODUCTION TO OUTBREAK DETECTION

Every undead outbreak, regardless of its size, has a beginning. Early detection and advance preparation will ensure your best chance for survival. This journal has several entry pages reserved for recording suspicious events that could indicate a possible outbreak. Examples include:

1 Homicides in which the victims were executed by head shots or decapitation.

2 Missing persons, particularly in wilderness or uninhabited areas.

3 Cases of "violent insanity" in which the subject attacked friends or family without the use of weapons. Find out if the attacker bit or tried to bite his victims.

4 Riots or other civil disturbances that began without provocation or other logical cause (such as racial tension, political actions, or legal decisions).

5 Disease-based deaths in which either the cause is undetermined or seems highly suspect. Be on the alert for suspicious explanations such as West Nile virus or mad cow disease. Either could be examples of a cover-up.

6 Any of the above in which media coverage was forbidden. An event that causes a government as media-conscious as our own to clamp down merits close attention.

Once an event has tripped your sensors, keep track of it. Note the location and its distance from you. Watch for similar incidents around or near the original site. Note the response of law enforcement and other government agencies. If they react more forcefully with each occurrence, chances are that an outbreak is unfolding.

SOLANUM: The Virus

Solanum works by traveling through the bloodstream from the initial point of entry to the frontal lobe of the brain. During this period, all bodily functions cease and the infected subject is rendered "dead." The brain, however, remains alive, while the virus mutates its cells into a completely new organ. The most critical trait of this new organ is its independence from oxygen. By removing the need for this all-important resource, the undead brain can utilize, but is in no way dependent upon, the complex support mechanism of the human body. This new organism is a zombie, a member of the living dead.

SUSPICIOUS EVENTS: Journal Entry

date:

time:

location:

distance from:

specifics:

action taken:

Develop the First Weapon

Americans are notorious for their bad diets, lack of exercise, and relentless fetish for labor-saving technology. As recognizable as the term "couch potato" is, a more accurate term would be "cattle": fat, lazy, listless, and ready to be eaten. Don't fall into this trap. Obey a strict diet and physical-fitness regimen. Concentrate on cardiovascular instead of strength-building exercise. When a situation does arise, you must know exactly what your body is capable of! The human body, if cared for and trained properly, is the greatest weapon on earth.

SUSPICIOUS EVENTS: Journal Entry

date:

time:

location:

distance from:

specifics:

action taken:

Plate Mail

The classic "suit of armor" conjures up images of
seemingly invincible knights dressed from head to
toe in shining steel. With so much protection,
wouldn't one be able to wander among the ranks
of the undead, taunting them with no danger of
repercussion? In truth, steel suits are heavy, cum-
bersome, suffocating, dehydrating, and extremely
noisy. Imagine five, ten, fifty attackers, all converg-
ing on your position, grabbing at the
plates, pulling them in all directions.
Without the speed to outrun
them or the agility to avoid
them, you will almost
certainly end up as
little more than
canned food.

SUSPICIOUS EVENTS: Journal Entry

date:

time:

location:

distance from:

specifics:

action taken:

Destroy Your Staircase!

As zombies are unable to climb, demolishing your
staircase basically guarantees your safety. No doubt
this will take time and energy, but it must be done.
Do not, under any circumstances, try to burn your
stairs away with the hope of controlling the fire.
Several people have attempted to save time in this
way; their efforts have ended in either death by fire
or the total destruction of their home. If you have a
ladder, use it to continue to stock your upstairs
refuge. If not, fill all sinks and other receptacles
with water, and prepare for a long wait.

SUSPICIOUS EVENTS: Journal Entry

date:

time:

location:

distance from:

specifics:

action taken:

WEAPONS: Chainsaw

Popular fiction has shown us the awesome, brutal power of the chain saw. How many horror movies have you seen in which this industrial killing machine has spelled doom for anyone and anything it touched? In reality, however, chain saws and similar powered devices rank extremely low on the list of practical zombie-killing weapons. Once drained of fuel, they provide as much protection as a handheld stereo. Another problem is noise. A chain saw's distinctive roar will be enough to broadcast to every zombie within earshot, "Dinner is served!"

SUSPICIOUS EVENTS: Journal Entry

date:

time:

location:

distance from:

specifics:

action taken:

ATTACK STRATEGY: Lure and Destroy

Use one or more vehicles to enter an infested area. Once inside, make as much noise as possible to draw the undead to you. Exit the area slowly, matching the speed of your pursuers. Like the Pied Piper, you will soon acquire a tail of zombies, a grisly parade slouching after you. At this point, sharpshooters posted at the back of the vehicles can proceed to take them down. The pursuing ghouls will not realize what is happening, as their primitive brains will not notice that their comrades are falling all around them.

SUSPICIOUS EVENTS: Journal Entry

date:

time:

location:

distance from:

specifics:

action taken:

Beware of Underwater Corpses

Never forget the possibility of ghouls stumbling into nearby water before you declare an area secure. Too often humans have repopulated "cleared" zones only to be attacked days, weeks, even months later by zombies who have just recently found their way back to dry land. Because the undead can exist, operate, and kill in a liquid environment, try to avoid wetlands altogether, or wade through only the shallowest water. Watch for ripples or any subsurface motion. A zombie might have sunk through the soft mud and may be trapped just below the waterline.

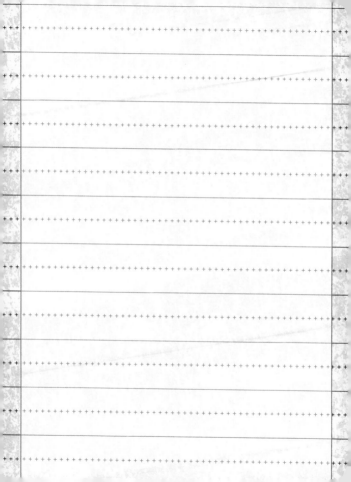

SUSPICIOUS EVENTS: Journal Entry

date:

time:

location:

distance from:

specifics:

action taken:

Bludgeons, Blades, and Other Handweapons

Imagination and improvisation are two invaluable assets during clashes with the living dead. By all means, feel free to regard all the materials around you as a cache of potential weapons. If you discover an implement or tool that you think might make a good weapon, ask yourself these questions:

1. Can it crush a skull in one blow?
2. If not, can it decapitate in said blow?
3. Is it easy to handle?
4. Is it light?
5. Is it durable?

Questions 3, 4, and 5 will have to depend on your present situation.

Questions 1 and 2 are essential!

Potter Style

Copyright © 2008

by Potter Style.

Based on the book *The Zombie Survival Guide:*

Complete Protection from the Living Dead by Max Brooks,

published by Three Rivers Press, a division of Random House, Inc.

© 2003 by Max Brooks. Illustrations © 2003 by Max Werner.

www.clarksonpotter.com

Printed in China

ISBN: 978-0-307-40639-2